ADVERTISING

Bess Milton

Children's Press®
A Division of Scholastic Inc.
New York / Toronto / London / Auckland / Sydney
Mexico City / New Delhi / Hong Kong
Danbury, Connecticut

Book Design: Mindy Liu and Michael DeLisio
Contributing Editor: Eric Fein
Photo Credits: Cover © Lester Lefkowitz/Corbis; p. 4 © Mark Peterson/Corbis Saba;
p. 7 © KJ Historical/Corbis; pp. 8, 10 © Corbis; p. 13 © Museum of the City of New
York/Corbis; p. 15 © PEMCO-Webster&Stevens Collection; Museum of
History&Industry, Seattle/Corbis; pp. 16, 18, 22 © Bettmann/Corbis; pp. 21, 27
© Milan Ryba/Globe Photos, Inc.; pp. 25, 28, 34, 36, 41 © AP/Wide World Photos;
p. 30 © Ralf-Finn Hestoft/Corbis Saba; p. 39 © Neema Frederic/Corbis Sygma

Library of Congress Cataloging-in-Publication Data

Milton, Bess.
    Advertising / Bess Milton.
    p. cm.—(American pop culture)
    Summary: Explores how advertising both reflects and shapes popular
    culture in America.
    Includes bibliographical references and index.
    ISBN 0-516-24075-7 (lib. bdg.) — ISBN 0-516-25943-1 (pbk.)
    1. Advertising—Juvenile literature. 2. Advertising—United
    States–Juvenile literature. [1. Advertising. 2. Popular culture—United
    States.] I. Title. II. Series.

HF5829.M55 2003
659.1'042'0973—dc22

                                      2003011996

        1 2 3 4 5 6 7 8 9 10 R 13 12 11 10 09 08 07 06 05 04

Contents

Introduction   5

1 Early Advertising   9

2 Selling to America   23

3 The Importance of
   Character   29

4 The Future of
   Advertising   35

New Words   42

For Further Reading   44

Resources   45

Index   47

About the Author   48

New York City's Times Square is an example of how advertising has become an important part of American culture.

Introduction

You are standing in Times Square, in the center of New York City. Bright lights surround you. Everywhere you turn, there are flashing signs. Some of the signs are as tall as the skyscrapers on which they hang. The signs are advertisements for hundreds of different products. Colorful words and images fight for your attention. Your eyes can't stop at just one sign. You wonder how advertising got to be this powerful.

The answer is deep in the heart of American culture—the American dream. Americans want the best of everything. They generally consume, or buy and use, a lot of goods. The American spirit is one that strives for excellence in how we live and how we work. This is also true of the products and services we buy. We work hard to make good lives for ourselves and our families. When the work is done, we like to enjoy ourselves. One of the ways we determine what we want is through advertising. Advertising is the way product manufacturers give people information about their products in the hope they will buy them. Advertising comes in many different forms. Coupons, posters, and television commercials are just some of the kinds of advertising used.

Advertisers know that people not only want products they will enjoy, but also ones that will help them be safe, secure, and healthy. Advertisers also appreciate people's emotional needs. We need to feel loved, that we belong, and are important. Advertisers understand this and design their ads to address these needs so that we will buy their products.

Over the years, advertising has become more than just selling products. Advertising has become an important part of American popular culture. The very best ads represent American values and beliefs. These are the ads that last through generations. They help us understand America's past—and give a look into our future.

Advertising is used for more than getting people to buy a product. It can also be used to motivate people to take action. This poster from World War II was used to urge Americans to help the war effort.

This ad was used in the 1850s by the American Soap Company. The picture on the left shows how hard it was for the woman in the drawing to wash clothes. The picture on the right shows how much easier wash day became once the woman began to use this advertiser's product.

Early Advertising

American advertising dates back to the time of the American Revolutionary War (1775–1783). The American colonies won the war against England and became the United States of America. Until this time, most products used by the colonists were made in England. These products were brought to America on ships. After the war, it was important to get Americans to buy American-made products. Having Americans buy these products had a good effect on the country. It helped the nation's businesses grow and made

This 1857 poster advertised a railroad service that ran from New York City to Vermont.

the economy stronger. Businesspeople used tools such as signs and posters to advertise that their products were American-made. "Buying American" also created a sense of pride in Americans. Manufacturers often used pride in the country as a selling point for their product. To this day, people usually associate any product marked "Made in America" with being of high quality.

By the turn of the century, the country was steadily developing. Americans headed west and the United States grew. In the mid-1800s, the age of railroad travel began. Miles and miles of tracks stretched across the United

States. This created a way for goods produced in the east to get to all parts of the nation. Transporting the goods was useless, however, unless people all over the country wanted to buy them.

During the mid-nineteenth century, nearly a thousand newspapers were being printed across the country. This provided manufacturers with the opportunity to reach many people in many places. Newspaper printers began to sell parts of a page to different companies, allowing them to advertise their products to the entire nation.

A Business Begins

In 1843, Volney C. Palmer, a salesman from Philadelphia, opened a business as a "middle-man" between the newspapers and the manu-facturers. He was the very first advertising agent. Palmer charged the newspaper owners a fee to find manufacturers willing to adver-tise in their papers. Palmer was successful, but unpopular. As soon as the ad was placed, he considered his job done. He never stuck around long enough to guarantee sales for the manufacturers. He also did not make sure the newspaper owners were paid for their page space by the manufacturers. Although Palmer's behavior caused mistrust toward the area of advertising, ad agents began to pop up all over the country.

In New Hampshire in the late 1860s, George P. Rowell came up with a plan that would fix Palmer's problem. Rowell realized that no company would continue to advertise unless the ads made them a profit. Rowell researched newspapers, hoping to find out what kind of people read them. He then advised the advertisers on how to promote their products. Rowell believed honesty was always the best way to make a sale. He encouraged his clients to truthfully point out the best features of their goods.

Within a few years, advertising agents were no longer just middlemen between newspapers and manufacturers. Inspired by Rowell's success, they took on the role of creating ad

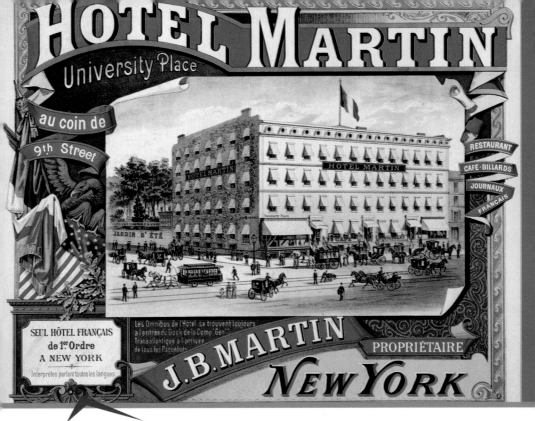

As printing technology improved, so did the design and artwork of most advertising. This beautifully illustrated ad for the Hotel Martin in New York City is from 1884.

campaigns for their clients. Ad campaigns were the ideas used to sell products. When printing equipment and techniques improved, so did the design of ad styles. By the early 1900s there were many ad agencies. Now broken up into design, writing, and business divisions, manufacturers eagerly hired these new advertising businesses.

Beginning of Brands

By the late 1800s, Americans did most of their shopping at general stores. General stores sold everything from food to soap to clothing. There were very few brand-name products. No one went shopping for a particular name brand of soap. People bought any soap the general store had.

However, by the mid-1800s, brand names and logos started to appear on products. In 1852 a company began selling blank paper sacks to other companies for packaging their products. Advertising agencies, also known as ad agencies, saw these sacks as an ideal place to put each company's name. Brand-name packaging was born. The way Americans shopped began to change. Consumers had choices to make about which brand of soap to buy.

Advertising agents introduced flashy packaging to help convince people to buy their client's brand. People quickly developed favorites. If general store owners wanted to stay in business, they now had to sell the brands their customers demanded.

General stores were the main sources of supplies for most Americans in the 1800s and early 1900s. These stores saw their profits go up when they stocked their customers' favorite brand-name products.

Did You Know ?

RECENT STUDIES FROM THE MARKETING INDUSTRY HAVE DETERMINED THAT A PERSON'S BRAND LOYALTY MAY BEGIN TO FORM WHEN HE OR SHE IS AS YOUNG AS TWO YEARS OF AGE.

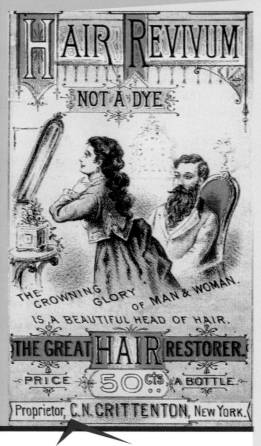

This trade card from around 1870 offers buyers of the product "a beautiful head of hair" for only fifty cents a bottle!

Trade Cards and Magazines

After brand names were established, companies wanted to spread news of their products as widely as possible. Newspapers had proven useful in reaching people within certain areas. However, most newspapers were sold only in small areas, not countrywide. To solve the problem, ad agencies began developing trade cards. Trade cards were postcard-sized and had a colorful picture on them, such as a building or bridge. Sometimes advertisers would put American symbols, such as the Statue of Liberty or Uncle Sam, on their trade cards. On the flip side of the card would be the advertiser's sales message. The product-makers sent the trade cards to local storeowners all over the nation. As the storeowners handed the cards out to their customers, a product's nationwide audience was formed. The colorful cards became so popular that some shoppers even started collecting them.

Ad agencies began to look for better ways to promote products across the country. In 1883, a magazine publisher named Cyrus Curtis and his wife Louisa found a solution. Most magazines printed at this time were expensive and geared toward men. These magazines did not include any ads. Cyrus and Louisa decided to create a new magazine, *Ladies' Home Journal.* They filled it with articles about topics such as family life and cooking. Each issue also overflowed with advertisements for household products, such as food and cleaning products. The magazine was an incredible advertising tool. Other magazines quickly followed in its successful footsteps.

Radio programs were expensive to make because they required a lot of highly trained people and special equipment.

Changing Technology

The first half of the twentieth century brought a new twist to the world of advertising. This time period saw the invention of radio and television within years of each other. From the moment they were introduced, both became very popular with Americans. It should be noted, however, that radios were easier and cheaper to buy than televisions.

The Radio

Radio allowed people to hear all kinds of programs, such as news, music, sports, and plays. Making these radio programs cost a lot of money. During radio's early days, commercials were not allowed to be broadcast. However, laws were soon changed. Radio show producers were allowed to seek out sponsors to pay for the production of the programs.

Advertisers were very willing to foot the bill for a radio show, since they could mention their products at the start and finish of each program's broadcast. The laws were changed yet again and ads were allowed during breaks in the programs. As listeners tuned in week after week and heard, "This show brought to you by…," they learned about many products on the market.

The Television

By the middle of the twentieth century, radio gave way to television. Television had an even greater impact on Americans. It affected the way people lived, worked, and even how they thought. Advertisers quickly began to use television as a way of promoting and selling their products and services. Americans loved the TV stars they watched each night. Ad agents put that love to good use. They hired the stars to appear in short TV commercials, called spots. Advertisers used these spots to promote various products and to show how to use them. The American audience trusted these celebrities because they saw so much of them. The spots were very successful. The age of the TV commercial had begun.

Did You Know ?

THE TERM "SOAP OPERA" COMES FROM THE FACT THAT EARLY RADIO MELODRAMAS WERE SPONSORED BY SOAP COMPANIES.

Super Ads

The NFL Super Bowl is one of the biggest TV events of the year. Each year, the Super Bowl attracts about eighty to ninety million television viewers. This fact is not lost on advertisers. With such a large audience, advertisers spend close to three million dollars to be able to air just one thirty-second commercial!

Actual color photograph of 1947 Studebaker Regal De Luxe Land Cruiser

Here's your style leader and star performer...
1947's thrill car...the postwar Studebaker!

Men of conscience as well as competence build long life into every Studebaker— The Studebaker craftsmen pictured are the Millers—S. R. and N. T. A 63-year-old father and 40-year-old son, they're old-timers on their Studebaker jobs. For over 95 years, there has been a steady sequence of these father-and-son teams at Studebaker.

Most people know that there's just one show-piece among today's cars. You see it pictured here. It's the postwar Studebaker.

This is the fresh, new kind of style that people hoped to see in all automobiles by now.

The daringly different design of this postwar Stude-baker is in the best of good taste. And quite as thrilling as its low-swung beauty is the way it rides and handles.

This is due to the sensa-tionally advanced chassis en-gineering of this Studebaker. All of the car's weight is poised in almost ideal balance.

Brightest star of the superb new postwar Studebaker line is the ultra-luxurious, extra-long-wheelbase Land Cruiser pictured above.

It's a photogenic dream car that proudly leads a Stude-baker fashion show of equally distinctive Champions and Commanders.

Give yourself a treat to re-member. See these postwar thrill cars now at a nearby Studebaker showroom.

STUDEBAKER
The postwar leader in motor car style

The Studebaker Corp'n, South Bend 27, Ind., U.S.A.

This ad for the 1947 Studebaker shows the new stylings of postwar automobiles. During the war, the Studebaker company made aircraft engines for the U.S. military.

Chapter 2

Selling to America

The Great Depression (1929–1939) and
World War II (1939–1945) forced people to
do without many of the comforts and products they had grown used to. However, after
the war, people wanted to put the hard times
behind them. They wanted to settle down,
have families, and enjoy peacetime.

Advertisers were more than happy to let
people know about all the new products and
services that could help Americans live better.
Advertising let people know about the latest
trends in foods, fashion, cars, and homes.

There are many creative ways to sell products to the public. Through the years, different styles of advertising have led to many memorable ads. These ads are so powerful—each in their own way—they have become a part of American popular culture. Let's take a look into the past to see how manufacturers sold their products to Americans.

She's Not Real?

In 1921, the Gold Medal baking flour company started receiving questions from customers about baking. The company wanted to develop a relationship with these customers so they would keep buying its products.

Executives at the company came up with a plan. They created an imaginary "kitchen expert" to answer the customers' letters. They named her Betty Crocker, a name chosen because it sounded friendly.

Betty quickly became a superstar, even though everything from her signature on the packaging to her picture was fake.

1936	**1955**	**1965**	**1968**
1972	**1980**	**1986**	**1996**

The face of Betty Crocker has changed over the years. These changes are made to keep the character of Betty current with the latest trends in women's fashion.

The company hired women to write cookbooks that were—and still are—sold with Betty's name. They even created a Betty Crocker line of food products, including cake mixes and icing. In 1924, a woman with a gentle voice was hired to play Betty on America's first radio cooking show, *Betty Crocker School of the Air.*

Americans trusted the company's products because they trusted Betty Crocker, the imaginary food expert. Although not real, she is a symbol of American homemaking values. The company set out to sell more baking flour. They ended up creating a piece of American popular culture.

Will You Marry Me?

Another type of advertising uses association. Using association, advertisers create a relationship between a product and something else—such as a feeling, a group of people, or even a time of day. If the ad campaign is successful, the public is reminded of the relationship each time they see that product. In 1948, the De Beers diamond company created an association campaign that grabbed the nation's attention—and has held it to this day.

The De Beers company wanted to sell more diamond rings. They hired an ad agency to come up with a clever way to do this. The result was the slogan, or phrase, "A Diamond is Forever." The slogan created a connection

De Beers uses stylish models to display their world-famous diamonds in its advertising.

between diamond rings and lifelong romance. Before this campaign, it was not common for a man to propose marriage by offering a woman a diamond. However, once the ads succeeded, it became an American tradition.

Some commercial characters take on a life of their own. This display shows some of Kellogg's most popular cereal characters: Snap, Crackle and Pop, Tony the Tiger, and Sam the Tucan.

The Importance of Character

During the 1940s, an advertising agent named Leo Burnett came up with a creative way to reach the American people. Burnett believed that pictures were the best way to send a message to consumers. He created what he called "commercial characters" to sell products. These characters were fun, lovable, and gave each product a personality.

One of the products Burnett worked on was a breakfast cereal for the Kellogg's company. The cereal was made from puffed grains of rice. Burnett discovered that when he

The Energizer Bunny has become so popular that he now makes personal appearances. People line up to get their picture taken with the bunny at places such as sporting events.

added milk to the cereal, it made sounds—it snapped, crackled, and popped. Based on these sounds, he created three characters named Snap, Crackle, and Pop. From that moment on, every box of the noisy cereal—named Rice Krispies—featured the characters. America quickly fell in love with them. Burnett's company created many other characters, including the Pillsbury Doughboy, the Jolly Green Giant, and Frosted Flakes' Tony the Tiger. The Burnett characters were popular because they did more than just sell products—they captured America's heart.

A Step Further

In 1989, an ad agency took Burnett's idea of commercial characters to a new level. They decided that if characters were good at grabbing America's attention, a character proving what a product could do would be even better. The ad agency was working on a campaign for a battery company that wanted to stand out from its competitors. To the buyer, most brands of batteries look similar. The agency had to come up with a way to convince America that their client's brand was special.

They came up with a character that would show America just how long the batteries could last. The character they invented was the Energizer Bunny, a cute windup toy. The fuzzy pink rabbit marched across TV screens while wearing sunglasses and playing a drum. The rabbit was successful. He just kept "going and going and going," right into the next decade. The Energizer Bunny made Americans believe that Energizer batteries would last— and showed the advertising world what a product demonstration could do for sales.

Nothing But the Truth

Advertising has changed over the years. However, one simple sales method has remained an industry favorite—the truth. A simple, honest statement about a product has proven to boost sales time and again.

In 1954, a candy company used the truth to bring their product into the public eye. The company had a new type of candy that was chocolate in the center with a colorful candy shell outside. The hard outer shell was special because it kept the chocolate from melting in your hand. An ad campaign was built on this simple fact, with a slogan Americans still love to this day: "M & Ms melt in your mouth, not in your hands."

Slogans

Slogans have been a favorite way to sell products since the beginning of advertising. A slogan is a statement or phrase that sends people a clear message about a product. If the slogan catches on, people begin to associate that message with the product. In the 1990s, the Nike Company's ad agency came up with a slogan for a new sneaker that did just that. The phrase "Just Do It" helped Nike sell sneakers and other products to people across America.

Nike used TV commercials featuring strong, athletic Americans involved in difficult sports. The people worked hard and always triumphed—they just "did it." The slogan was a hit. It emphasized the American ideal that through hard work, people could do anything. The commercials clearly presented an American value—and sold an enormous number of sneakers in the process.

Did You Know?

THE AVERAGE CHILD IS THOUGHT TO SEE MORE THAN 20,000 COMMERCIALS EVERY YEAR! THIS BREAKS DOWN TO ABOUT FIFTY-FIVE COMMERCIALS A DAY.

The Internet has opened up a variety of possibilities for advertising. Conventions are held on a regular basis for people who create and use Internet technology.

The Future of Advertising

The future of advertising will reflect the future of America. As events take place and American culture changes, advertising will change as well. As in the past, developments in technology will provide advertisers with new ways to reach the public.

The Internet

The Internet has become a part of everyday life in America. It began in 1969 as a research network for the United States military, but has become a central part of American culture.

The Internet is not only an important advertising tool, but allows people to shop online from the comfort of their homes.

Many people now spend as much time surfing the Web as they do watching television. They can spend time in chat rooms meeting people, reading magazines, doing research, using E-mail, and shopping online. As the Internet became popular, companies created Web sites from which to sell products. Advertisers had to then find a way to get people to visit these sites.

Banner Ads

Experts decided that the best way to get people to visit a site was to make it easy for them to get there. Typing in a long Web address might keep the public from going to a site. As a result, banner ads were developed. Known also as pop-up ads, these advertisements are boxes that appear as a person visits different Web sites. They are banners that stretch across the top, sides, or bottom of the screen. They offer quick links to other sites, where the person can buy products. Some of the ads actually pop up in new onscreen boxes.

While banner ads work, many people find them annoying. Now it is almost impossible to visit a Web site without facing multiple banner ads. Sometimes so many ads pop up that a computer may freeze, or stop working.

Advertisers thought that banner ads were the perfect way to profit from the Internet. They were sure that they had figured out how to use this modern technology to help sell products. Unfortunately, they didn't count on people disliking these types of ads.

Spreading the Word

Another popular way for companies to let the public know about their Web sites is to show them as often as possible. Everything from napkins to pizza boxes to billboards now advertise Web sites. Store cash registers often print these sites right on customer receipts. TV commercials display company sites and encourage people to visit them for more information on a product. Some even offer discounts or free products only to Web customers.

It is important for companies to let people know about their Web sites, in order to sell products. It is also a good way to let loyal customers know that the company is modern and growing alongside developing technology. The Internet has had a huge effect on American culture. Most companies want to make it clear to consumers that they haven't been left behind. They want to keep loyal customers who trusted them in the past just as much as they want to bring in new ones.

Ads for companies can be found almost anywhere—including the subway! This Microsoft.com ad was used in San Francisco, California, to get people to apply for jobs at the company.

Interactive Television

In the future, advances in technology will continue to change the advertising industry. New equipment that brings television and the

Did You Know ?

IN 2001, ADVERTISERS IN THE U.S. SPENT ABOUT 230 BILLION DOLLARS PROMOTING THEIR PRODUCTS.

Internet together will find its way into everyday life. This combination is called Interactive Television (ITV). Through ITV, audiences are involved in what happens onscreen. They can play along with game shows and even use remote controls to order products during commercials. This would give companies a whole new audience to advertise to: on-the-spot shoppers.

Some people don't believe this technology will become popular. They think that only very wealthy people will be able to afford the equipment, and therefore, see new trends in advertising. Others believe it will be a great success because the prices of new technology often drop quickly. They claim that many new advances are attacked when they first come out—including the Internet, which has certainly proven it is here to stay.

Interactive television will provide advertisers with a new audience of eager consumers in America and all over the world.

We may not know what the future holds for technology, but one thing is for sure: Advertising will always be a major part of American culture. From the fun characters that people fall in love with year after year, to commercials that feel like old friends, advertising has a unique way of capturing America's spirit.

New words

advertising (**ad**-ver-tize-ihng) an organized method of giving information about products and services being offered for sale

advertising agency (**ad**-ver-tize-ihng **ay**-juhn-see) a business where advertising agents work to give the public information about products companies want to sell

advertising agent (**ad**-ver-tize-ihng **ay**-juhnt) someone who works in advertising, giving the public information about products companies want to sell

association (uh-soh-see-**ay**-shuhn) a connection that you make in your mind

brand (**brand**) a particular make of a product

broadcast (**brawd**-kast) to send out a program on television or radio; a television or radio program

commercial (kuh-**mur**-shuhl) a television or radio advertisement; to do with buying and selling things

creative (kree-**ay**-tiv) good at using your imagination and thinking of new ideas

new words

demonstration (**dem**-uhn-stray-shuhn) a presentation of how to use something, such as a product

interactive (in-tur-**ak**-tiv) allowing users to make choices in order to control and change a program in some ways

Internet (**in**-tur-net) the electronic network that allows millions of computers around the world to connect together

loyal (**loi**-uhl) firm or faithful to one's country, family, friends, or beliefs

program (**proh**-gram) a television or radio show

slogan (**sloh**-guhn) a phrase or motto used by a business, a group, or an individual to express a goal or belief

sponsors (spon-**surz**) those who pay the costs of a radio or television broadcast in return for having their products advertised

Fleming, Robert. *The Success of Caroline Jones Advertising, Inc.: An Advertising Success Story.* New York: Walker & Company, 1996.

Mierau, Christina. *Accept No Substitutes: The History of American Advertising.* Minneapolis, MN: Lerner Publications Company, 2000.

West, Darrell M. *Air Wars: Television Advertising in Election Campaigns, 1952-1996.* Washington, D.C.: Congressional Quarterly Inc, 1997.

Organizations

American Association of Advertising Agencies
405 Lexington Avenue, 18th Floor
New York, NY 10174-1801
(212) 682-2500
www.aaaa.org

The Advertising Council, Inc.
261 Madison Avenue, 11th Floor
New York, NY 10016
(212) 922-1500
www.adcouncil.org

Resources

Web Sites

About Advertising

http://advertising.about.com

This Web site has links to many different advertising Web sites.

The Advertising Century

http://adage.com/century

This Web site presents a century of advertising in America. It includes the top people, slogans, and campaigns in the industry.

Advertising Educational Foundation

http://www.aef.com

This informative Web site is the home of the Advertising Educational Foundation. Learn about different styles of advertising (past and present) on this site.

InDex

A

advertising agent, 11–12, 14, 29

American Revolutionary War, 9

association, 26

B

brand, 14, 16, 31

broadcast, 19

C

celebrities, 20

characters, 29–31

commercial, 6, 19–21, 29, 31, 33, 38, 40–41

creative, 24, 29

Crocker, Betty, 24–25

D

De Beers, 26

demonstration, 32

G

Great Depression, 23

I

interactive, 40

Internet, 35–38, 40

L

Ladies' Home Journal, 17

loyal, 38

M

"Made in America", 10

magazines, 17, 36

InDex

N
newspapers, 11–12,
16

P
packaging, 14, 24
Palmer, Volney C., 11
programs, 19

R
radio, 18–19, 25
Rowell, George P., 12

S
slogan, 26, 32–33
sponsors, 19

About the Author

Bess Milton is a writer and editor living in New York.